CHRISTMAS SONGS

For HARP

ISBN 978-1-4803-9842-9

Hal•Leonard®
CORPORATION

7777 W. BLUEMOUND RD. P.O. BOX 13819 MILWAUKEE, WI 53213

Visit Hal Leonard Online at
www.halleonard.com

Feliz Navidad

Music and Lyrics by José Feliciano

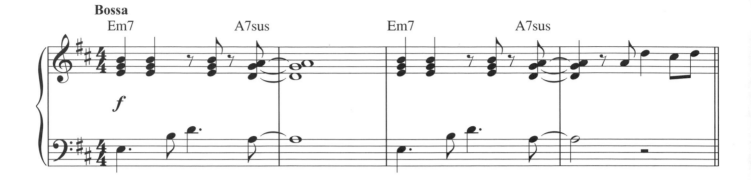

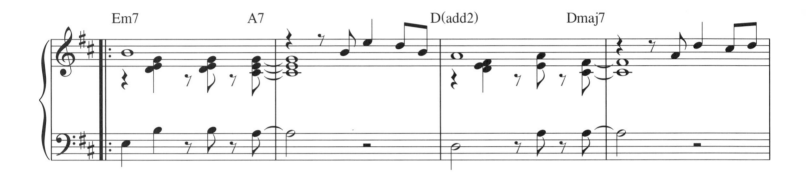

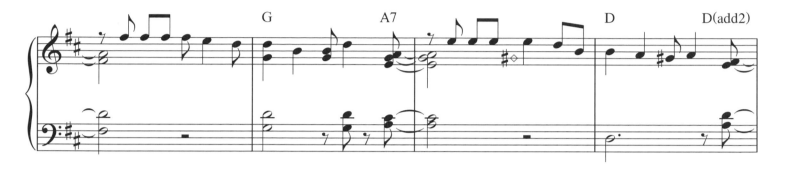

The First Noel

17th Century English Carol
Music from W. Sandys' *Christmas Carols*

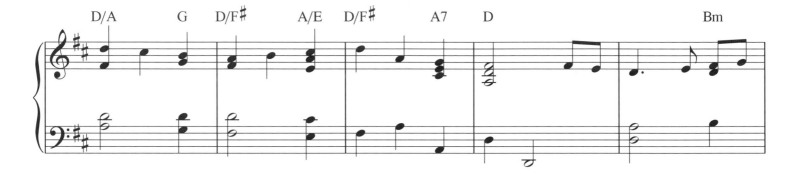

Frosty the Snow Man

Words and Music by Steve Nelson and Jack Rollins

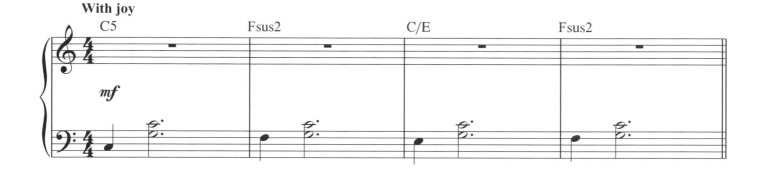

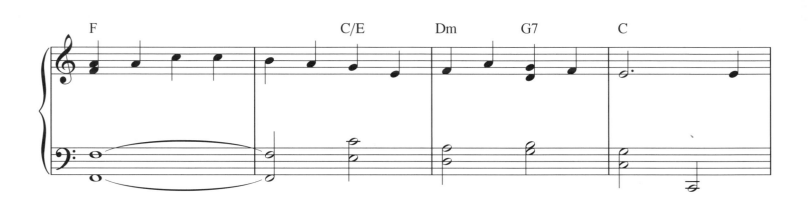

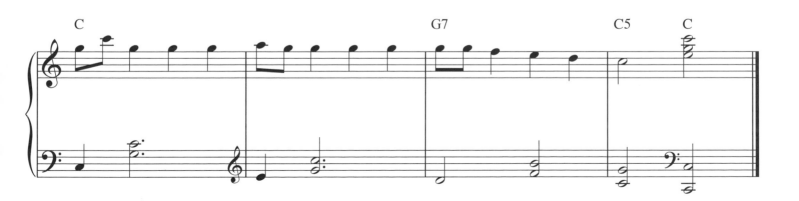

God Rest Ye Merry, Gentlemen

19th Century English Carol

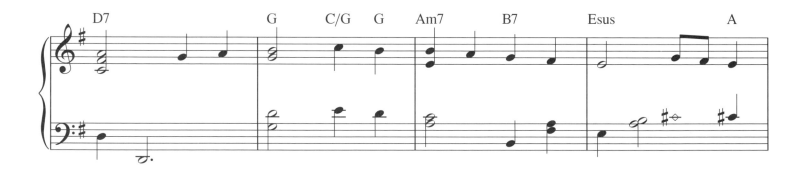

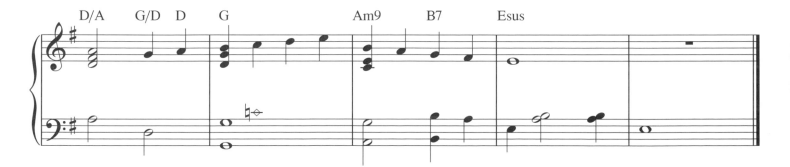

Good King Wenceslas

Words by John M. Neale
Music from *Piae Cantiones*

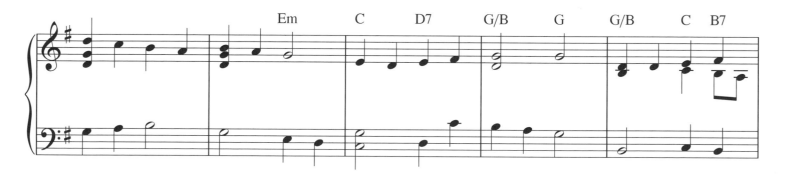

Have Yourself a Merry Little Christmas

from MEET ME IN ST. LOUIS

Words and Music by Hugh Martin and Ralph Blane

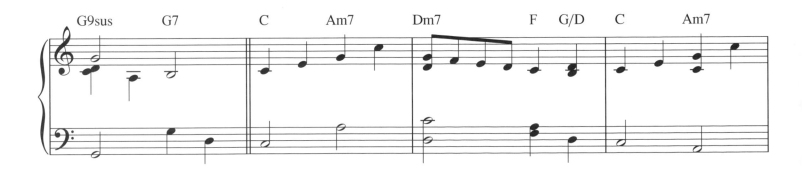

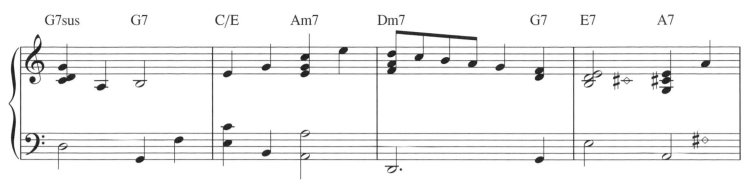

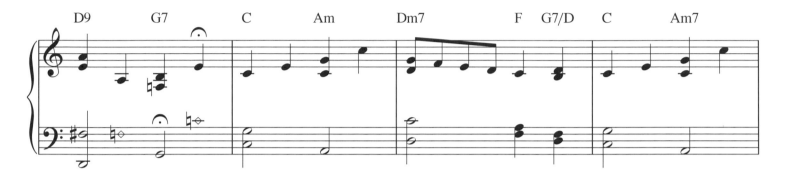

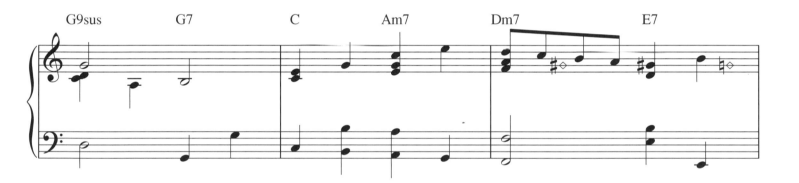

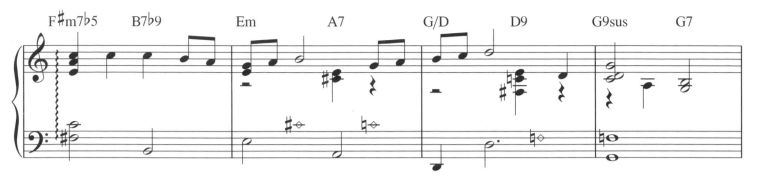

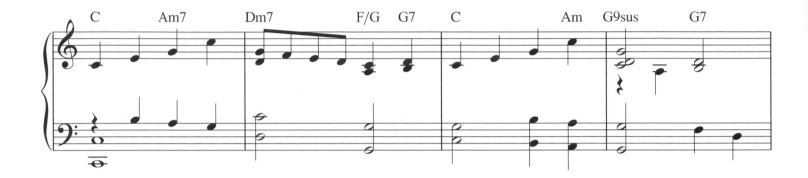

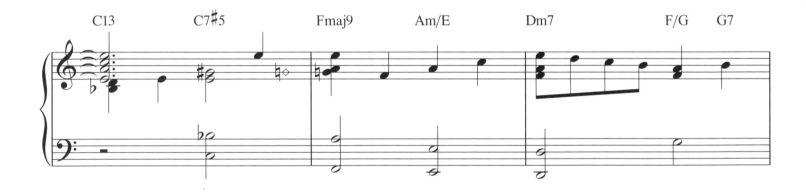

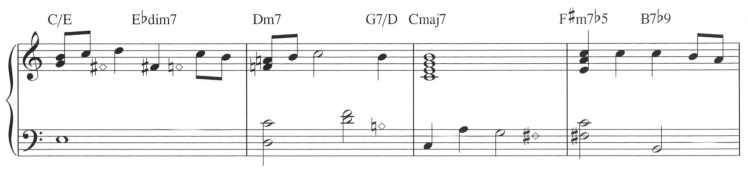

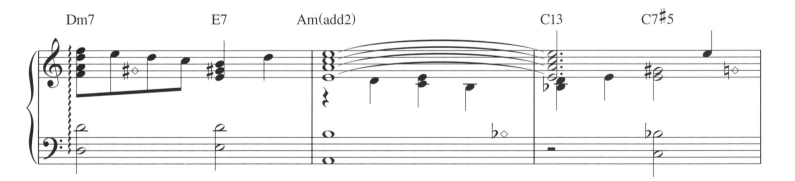

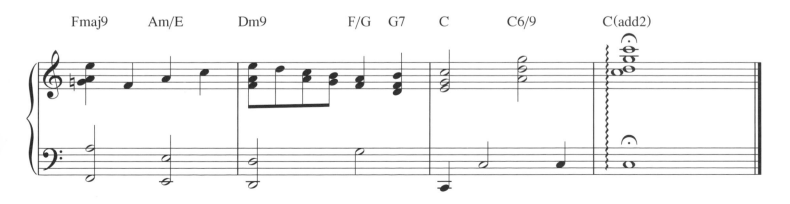

I Wonder as I Wander

By John Jacob Niles

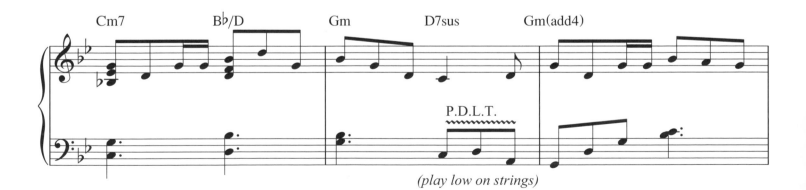

(play low on strings)

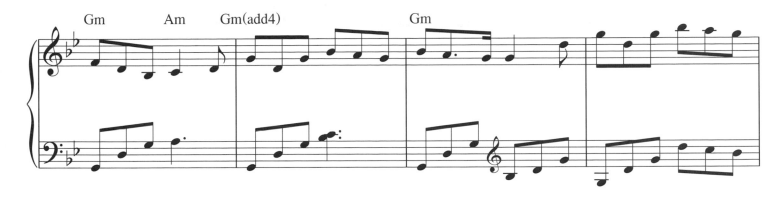

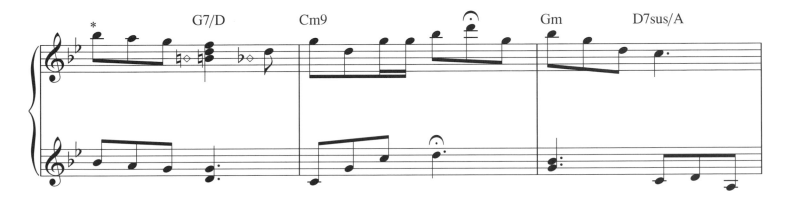

Helpful hint: lift lever with thumb while keeping hand in position.

I'll Be Home for Christmas

Words and Music by Kim Gannon and Walter Kent

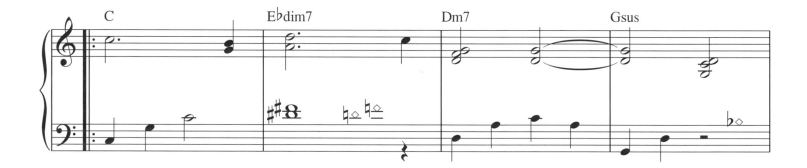

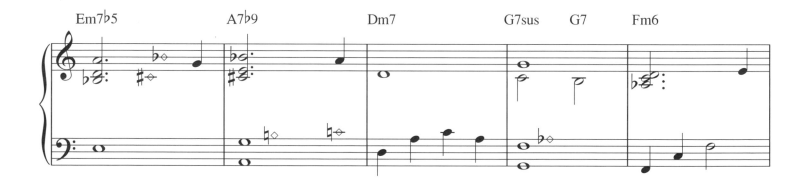

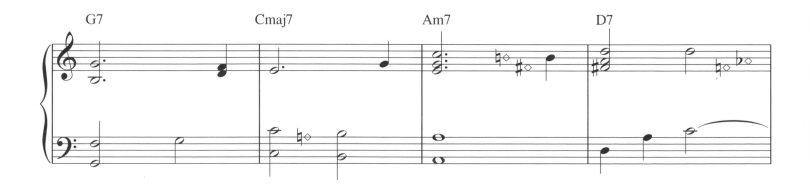

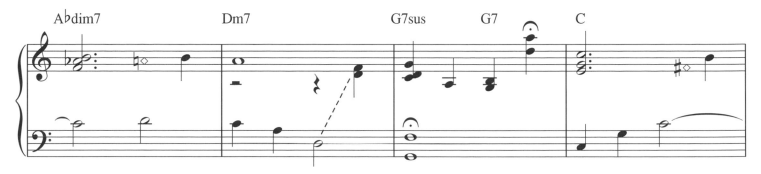

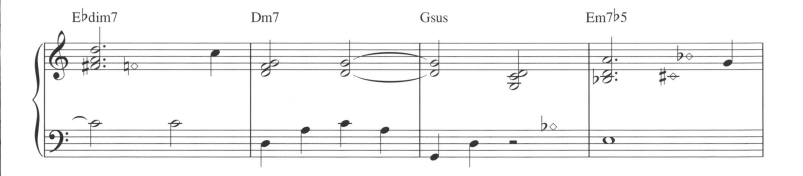

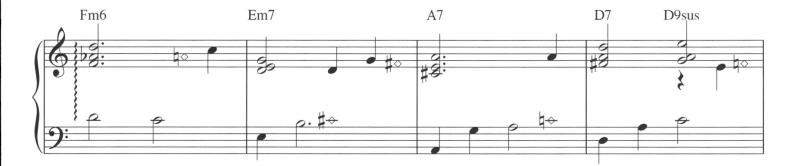

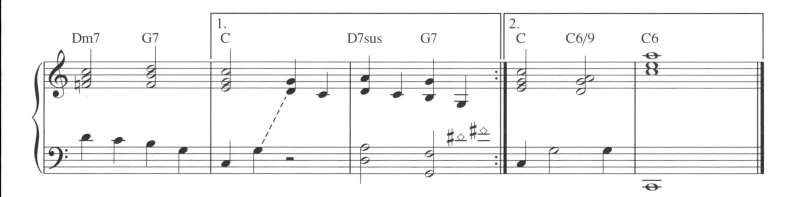

The Little Drummer Boy

Words and Music by Harry Simeone, Henry Onorati and Katherine Davis

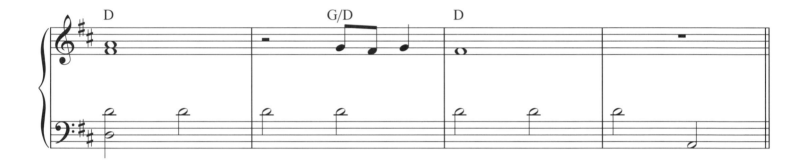

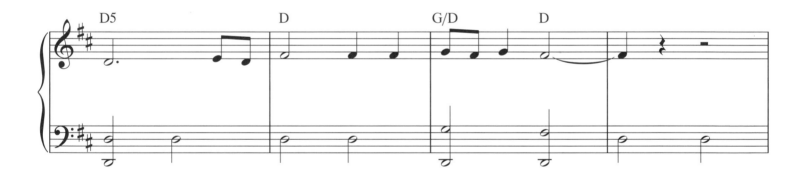

My Favorite Things

from THE SOUND OF MUSIC

Lyrics by Oscar Hammerstein II
Music by Richard Rodgers

Easy Waltz

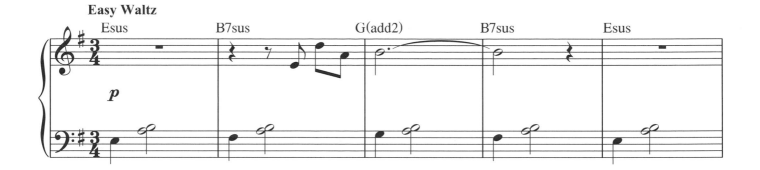

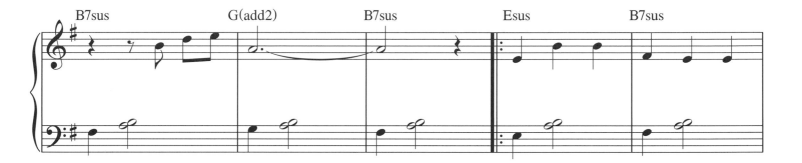

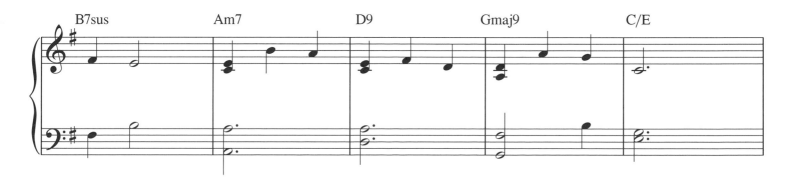

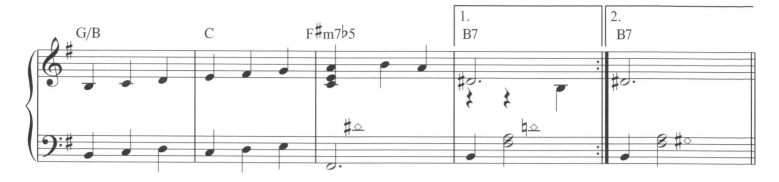

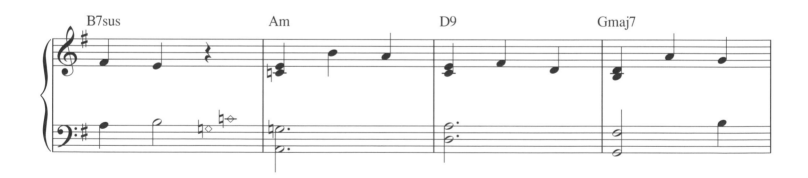

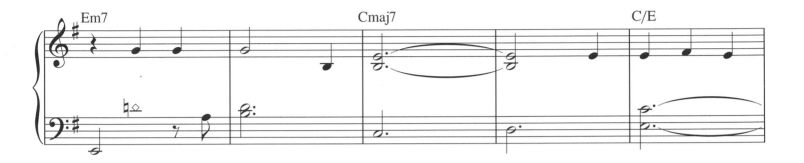

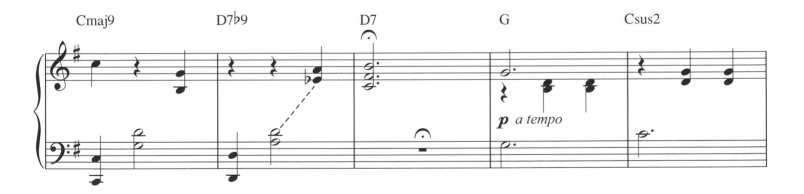

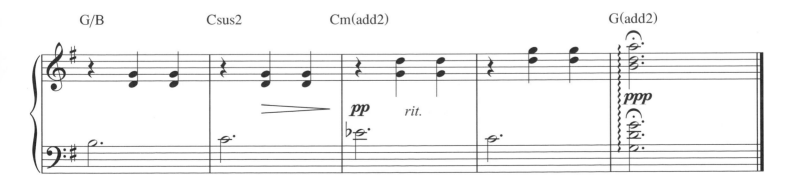

Rudolph the Red-Nosed Reindeer

Music and Lyrics by Johnny Marks

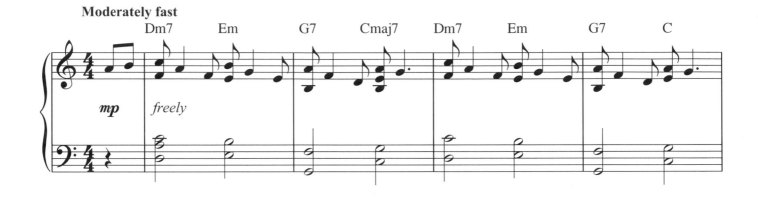

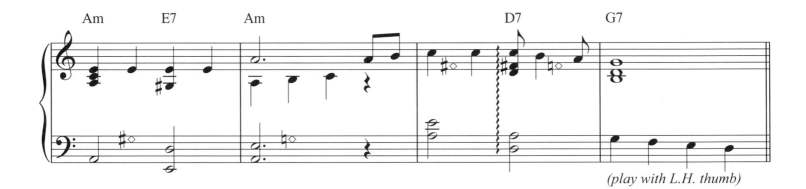

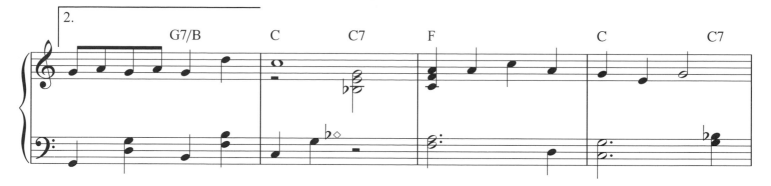

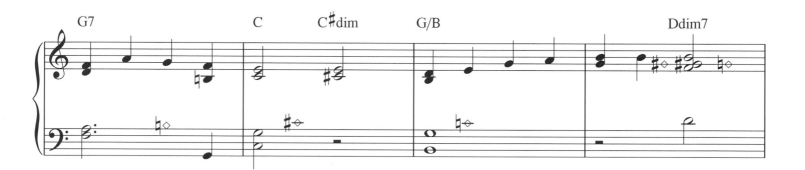

Silent Night

Words by Joseph Mohr
Translated by John F. Young
Music by Franz X. Gruber

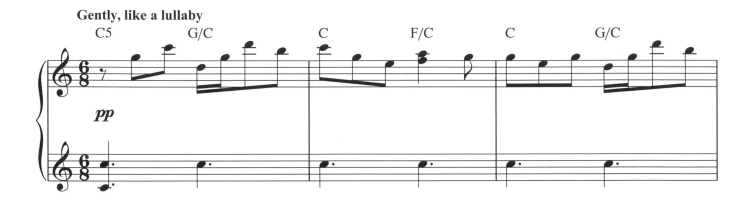

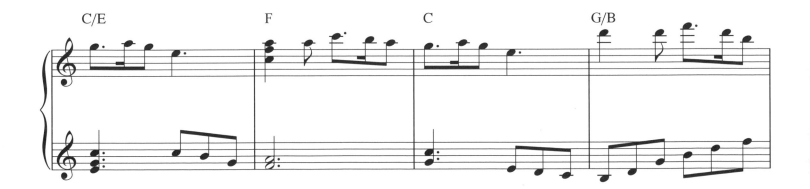

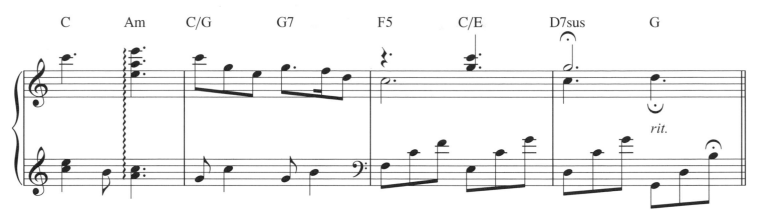

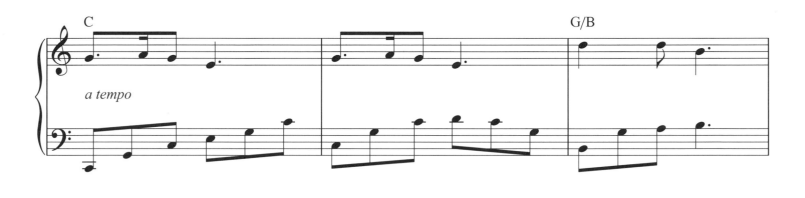

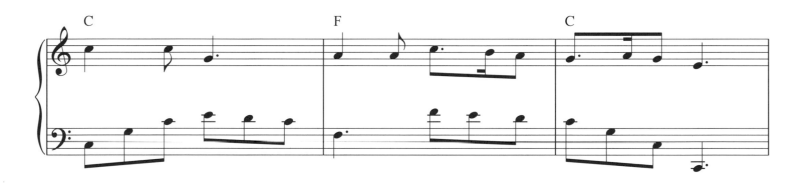

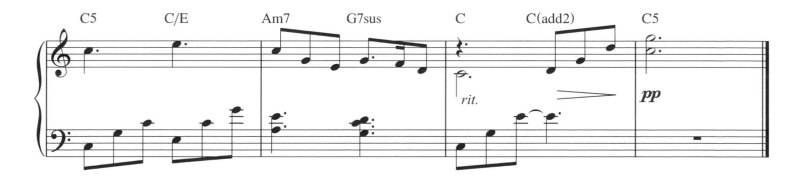

Silver and Gold

Music and Lyrics by Johnny Marks

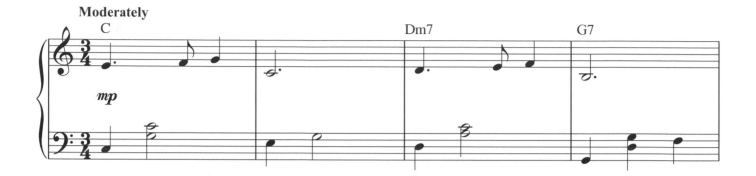

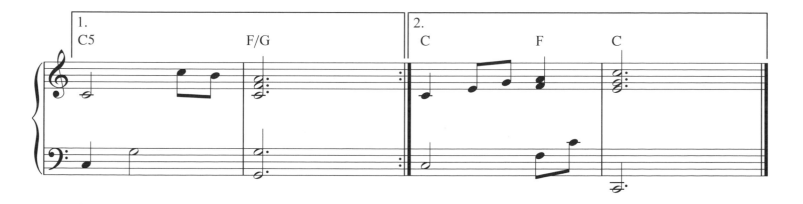

Silver Bells

from the Paramount Picture THE LEMON DROP KID

Words and Music by Jay Livingston and Ray Evans

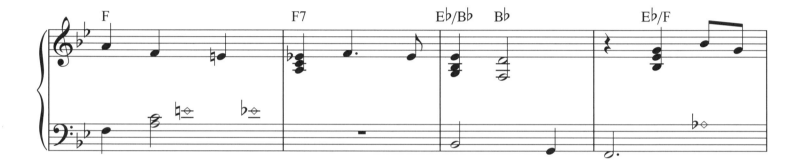

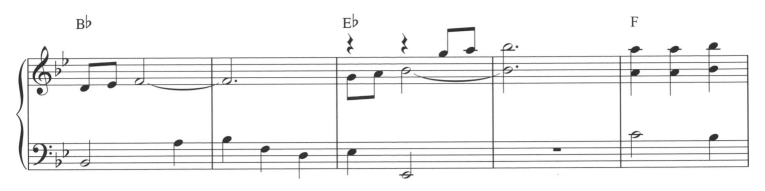

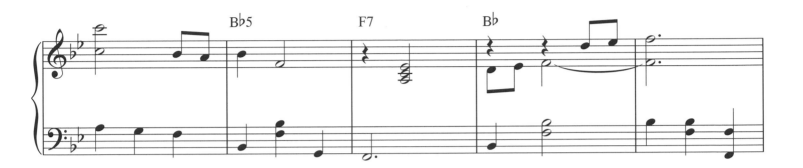

White Christmas

from the Motion Picture Irving Berlin's HOLIDAY INN

Words and Music by Irving Berlin

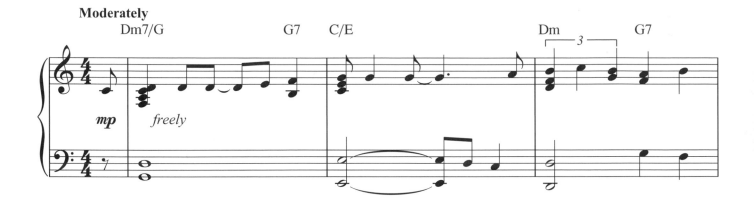

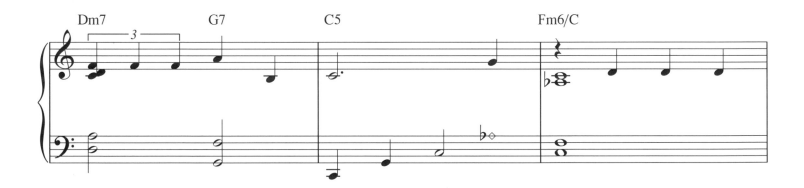

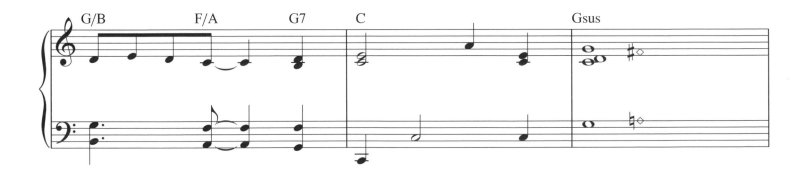

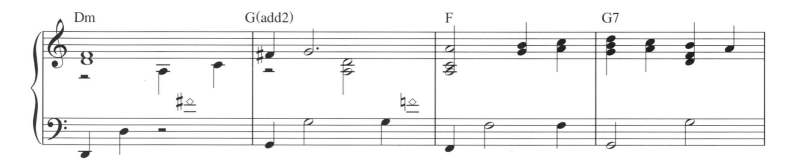

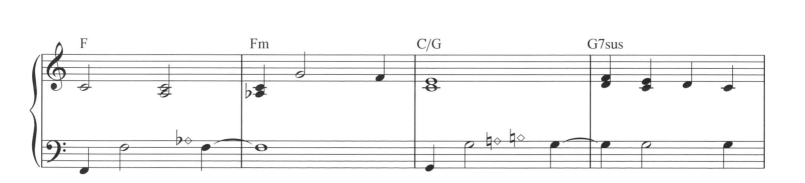

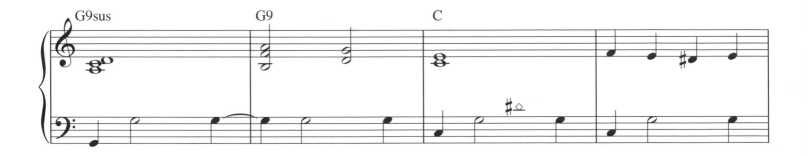

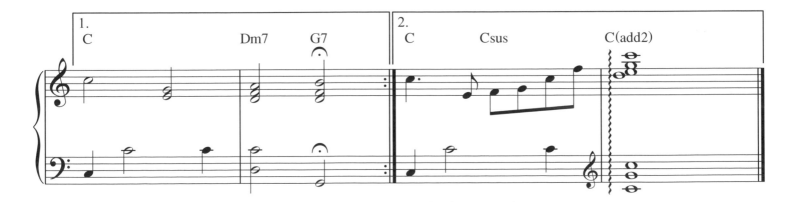

Winter Wonderland

Words by Dick Smith
Music by Felix Bernard

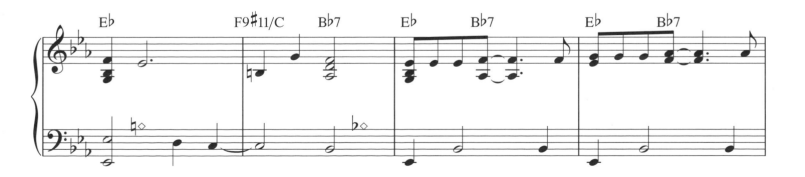

37

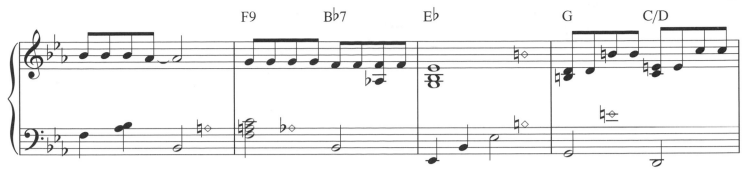

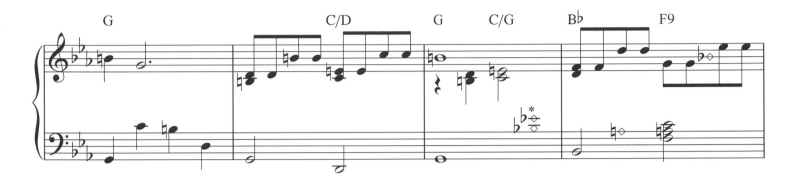

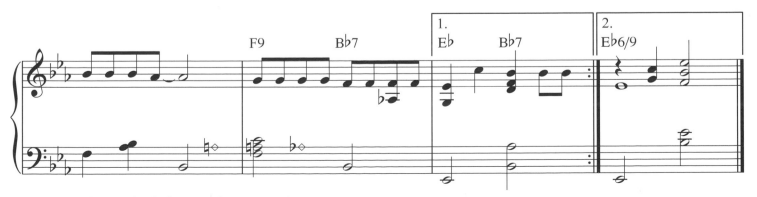

Note: push these both down at the same time.

The Christmas Song
(Chestnuts Roasting on an Open Fire)

Music and Lyric by Mel Tormé and Robert Wells

For this arrangement, tune your harp to D♭ major.
Except as noted in bar 1, begin with all D and G levers raised.

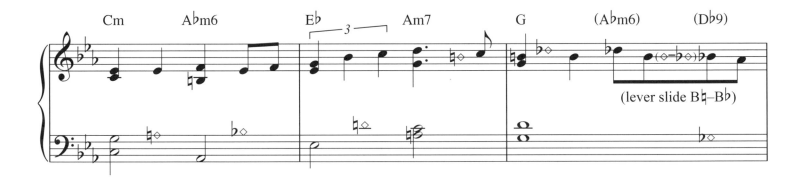

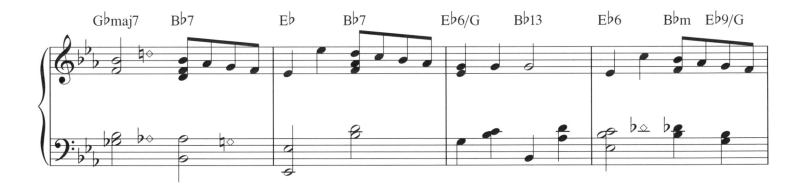

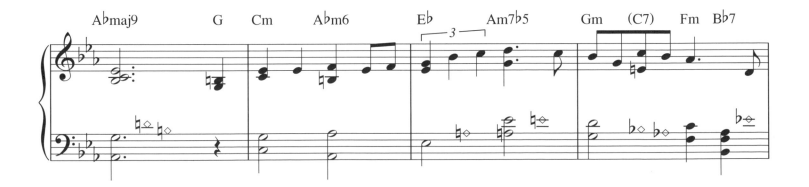

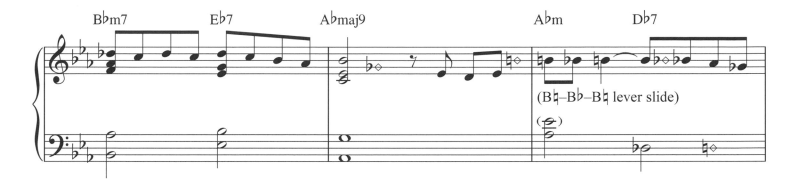

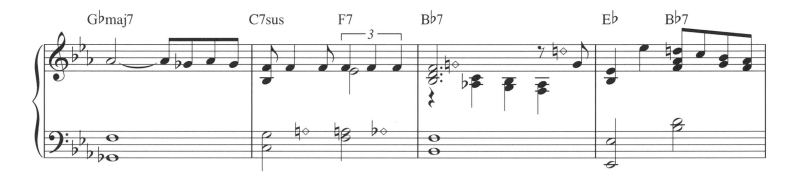